It's a Boy!

This edition published in 2015 by CWR, Waverley Abbey House, Waverley
Lane, Farnham, Surrey, GU9 8EP, UK. CWR is a Registered Charity – Number
294387 and a Limited Company registered in England – Registration Number
1990308.
First published in Great Britain in 2003 for Breakout Publishing by Verité CM
Ltd., Worthing, UK.
Breakout Publishing, PO Box 3070, Littlehampton, West Sussex, BN17 6WX, UK.
www.breakout.org.uk

ISBN: 978-1-78259-454-3
Printed in the UK by Linney Group

ALEXA TEWKESBURY

Alexa is the author of several storybooks for young children, including *Topz Secret Diaries*, *Topz Secret Stories*, and *Topz Gospels* series, the *Pens* Bible-reading series, the *Pens* and *Topz Activity Bibles*, as well as the screenplay for the film *My Month with Mrs Potter* (2015). Alexa is also a freelance copy editor and proofreader, as well as an actor and storyteller (see www.alexatewkesbury.com).

STEVE LEGG

Steve is an evangelist, author and founder of The Breakout Trust, a Christian mission organisation. For over 27 years he has travelled the world using a crazy mix of comedy, trickery and mystery to communicate the Christian message. His passion is creative communication of the reality of the Christian faith through performances, books, DVD's and other resources. The author of 13 books, much of his time is spent on the groundbreaking men's Christian lifestyle magazine, *Sorted*, which has 100,000 readers in 26 countries.

JULIAN TEWKESBURY

Julian began making cartoon films at the age of sixteen, and, in 1985, he and a friend started making puppet films for television. This culminated in employment at Jim Henson's Creature Shop in London, where he worked on the TV sitcom Dinosaurs. He was also involved in a pilot for the film *Dragonheart* (1996). Julian has now moved from puppetry to computer animation. The animated version of this book was first released in 2005 and since then Julian has been developing a number of projects for film and television, the most recent being a CGI sci-fi action adventure for the family audience (see www.tyhaan.com).

It's a Boy!

by Alexa Tewkesbury and Steve Legg

"Right, he's got another five minutes and that's it!" snapped Tommy. The agitated little quail was pacing up and down in the shade of a tree, stopping every few moments to scan the skies over Nazareth. The sun had risen hours ago and there was still no sign of Bobby, who'd flown off early in search of their breakfast. Tommy was starving. He glanced at his companion, who was calmly grooming herself with her beak.

"How can you just sit there, preening?" he asked.

Queenie shrugged. "A quail's got to look her best."

Before Tommy could reply, he was hit unexpectedly from behind by something round and brown that hurtled out of the sky and crash landed in an explosion of dust. He turned to see a dishevelled-looking quail proceed to pick himself up and shake dirt out of his ears.

"Bobby," said Tommy flatly, "what on earth do you think you're doing?"

"Getting breakfast," Bobby replied. He picked up a rather small, shrivelled object lying in the dust at his feet and placed it grandly in front of Tommy.

"There!" he announced proudly.

Tommy turned up his beak in disgust. "You mean you've been gone all this time and that's the best you could do?" he spluttered. "That's a wrinkled up old prune!"

"Do you mind?" Bobby answered indignantly. "I lost half my tail feathers nicking that!"

Queenie, apparently satisfied with her grooming, got up, shook out her feathers and without a word began to toddle across the dusty road.

"Where are you going?" called Tommy.

"*Someone's* got to get breakfast," she said, glancing back briefly and making her way towards a small, neat house on the other side of the road. An enticing smell of baking wafted through the downstairs window. Queenie fluttered up to the sill and peeped into the kitchen.

"There you are!" said a soft, friendly voice. "I was beginning to think you weren't coming." A young woman appeared at the window and broke up some bread onto the sill. Tommy and Bobby watched in stunned disbelief as Queenie began to tuck into the crumbs.

"How long's she been sneaking in there for breakfast?" asked Bobby hungrily.

"Beats me," Tommy answered. Then his face lit up. Queenie was beckoning to them with little jerks of her head. In seconds they'd scuttled across the road to join her. The bread was delicious – soft and warm, and fresh from the oven.

They were almost on the last beakful when a shattering crash sent them shooting nervously into the air. The young woman had dropped a large mixing bowl, which now lay in pieces on the floor. She stood in the middle of the room, terrified and surrounded by a sudden dazzling brightness. The quails froze. In front of her was an angel.

"Hello, Mary," he said. At the sound of his voice all three dived frantically for cover behind a stone jar in the corner of the room.

"How do you know my name?" Mary could scarcely speak. "What do you want?"

The angel smiled. "Don't look so worried," he said gently. "I'm Gabriel. God sent me to you."

"Would someone like to tell what in the fried fish is going on?" whispered Bobby hoarsely to Queenie and Tommy. But their eyes were fixed on the angel.

"Shhh!" they hissed.

Gabriel spoke again. "God thinks you're very special, Mary, and He's got a surprise for you. You're going to have a baby. A little boy."

Mary's eyes grew huge.

"You're to call Him Jesus," the angel went on. "He's the Son of God and will be a King to His people."

Mary could hardly breathe. "No, no!" She shook her head wildly. "There must be some mistake. I can't give birth to a King. I'm about to marry Joseph!"

"Have faith, Mary," answered Gabriel. "Nothing is impossible with God."

Queenie was sure she could hear Mary's heart thumping, and her own was pounding in her plump little chest. Breakfast had never been like this before.

She watched intently as Mary closed her eyes for a moment, then opened them and looked full into the angel's face.

"Then I am the Lord's servant," she said. "Let it be so."

The light faded and Gabriel vanished as suddenly as he had come.

Tommy broke the stunned silence. "Come on," he said softly. The quails fluttered up through the window and outside. But Queenie paused on the sill to look back. Mary was sitting quite still on a chair amidst the broken crockery, all thoughts of baking driven from her mind.

"I tell you what," said Bobby once they were all safely back under the tree, "I've seen some weird things in my time, but that ..."

Tommy looked thoughtfully at Queenie. "Do you think that angel really came from God?"

"Yes," she said, nodding, unable to take her eyes from Mary's window, "yes, I do." Tommy followed her gaze then glanced back at her anxious face.

"You don't have to worry," he said kindly. "Mary'll be all right. God's chosen her for this so He's not going to leave her. Besides, she's got Joseph. He'll look after her."

"That's right," added Bobby. "He'll look after *her* the way we look after *you*. We're a unit. And let's face it, no-one gets one over on *us*!"

But as Bobby finished speaking, a shadow fell across the three birds. They looked up. The gaunt, greasy face of King Herod's bird-catcher was smirking down at them.

"Move!" shrieked Tommy. But it was too late. A net landed squarely on top of them. They were trapped.

"Oh very nice!" gloated the catcher with a horrible, toothless grin. "You'll fatten up lovely for the royal table!" Then he scooped up the net, slung it over his shoulder and headed back to the palace.

"Watch it!" complained Tommy as he was shaken out into a large cage hanging up in Herod's vast throne room. Queenie bounced out next and Bobby landed on his head close to the bird-catcher's leering face.

"If my breath smelt like yours," he grimaced, reeling back, "I'd keep my mouth shut!"

A second, much fatter face appeared at the cage door. It belonged to King Herod. He patted the catcher on the back with a pudgy, ring-bedecked hand.

"Excellent!" he murmured, his voice rich and oily. "Start feeding them up, then go and fetch me some more."

The bird-catcher nodded greedily. "No sooner said than done, your Majesty."

He was as good as his word. Over the next few months, more and more quails were captured and tossed into the cage for fattening.

And fatten up they did, especially Bobby.

"There's one thing about being caught by a King," he mumbled one day, his beak crammed with cake, "at least you get to eat like one!"

"And then you get eaten *by* one!" muttered Tommy irritably.

"That's why we've got to get out," snapped Queenie, who was huddled fretfully in a corner. "But we've tried," Tommy moaned.

"Then we'll have to keep on trying," she persisted. "I'm not ready to be someone's dinner." She paused for a moment, then sighed quietly. "Besides, I want to see Mary. If she's having a baby it must be nearly time. I need to know she's all right."

It *was* nearly time. Back in Nazareth, Mary and Joseph had everything prepared for their new arrival. Then one morning they were given news that Emperor Caesar was ordering a massive census. Everyone had to go back to the town where they were born so they could be counted. They had no choice but to pack up what they could and make the long journey to Bethlehem. Fortunately, Mary was able to travel on their donkey. With her baby's birth so close, she could never have walked that far.

They arrived in Bethlehem late at night and quite exhausted. The town was packed with people already there for the census. Joseph called at several inns for a room but they were all full. Mary's face was anxious and drawn.

"It'll be all right," he said, taking her hand, "there's bound to be somewhere."

Mary tried to smile. She knew she was in God's hands but this wasn't at all how she'd imagined things.

It wasn't what Queenie was imagining either. She was fast asleep with the others, dreaming of freshly baked breadcrumbs and Mary gently rocking her new baby in a little wooden cradle in the kitchen.

The cage was suddenly jolted violently. All the birds woke with a start and began to flap and squawk. Then they saw Herod, his face thrust close to the bars and a nasty smile twisting his fat, slimy lips.

"I'm sorry," he said mockingly, as he enjoyed the alarm in their faces and their frightened, twitching eyes, "did I disturb you?" He laughed horribly and gave the cage another shake.

"Psycho!" muttered Bobby under his breath.

A herald entered the throne room.

"Some visitors to the royal court, your Majesty. They request an audience with you."

Herod waved him away and wandered over to a golden perch where his two pet falcons were hunched side by side. He put out a finger to stroke them.

"Oh, not today. Tell them I'm busy executing peasants or something."

The herald hesitated, looking uncomfortable.

"I would do, your Majesty, only… I think you might be interested in why they're here. They're looking for a new king."

Herod turned abruptly. "A new king?" he snapped. "There is no new king. Very well, you'd better send them in."

The herald disappeared and Herod turned back to his falcons, smoothing their feathers fondly.

"Can it be," he mused, "that someone's after my throne? How very unfortunate. For *him*!"

There were three visitors. As they came in they seemed very excited.

"Nice dress sense," remarked Bobby, whose interest was piqued enough to draw his attention briefly away from the overflowing feed tray.

"We spend a lot of time studying the skies, your Majesty," one of them explained, "and recently a particularly bright star appeared, announcing the birth of a new king."

"How fascinating!" simpered Herod. "So this new king is just a baby."

Queenie pricked up her ears.

"Yes," replied the man. "He might not even be born yet, and we've no idea where to find him."

Herod thought for a moment. "I tell you what," he said smugly, "I have some scholars who are wonderful at sorting out things like this. One of the perks of being a king. I'm sure they'll be able to help." Then he motioned his visitors to sit down and sent the herald to question his scholars.

"Did you hear that?" hissed Queenie, who'd become quite agitated.

"What?" said Tommy.

"The new king's a baby," she answered excitedly. Tommy and Bobby looked at each other blankly.

"Think about Mary," she persisted.

"That angel said *her* baby was going to be a King."

"So?" replied Bobby.

"So," exploded Queenie, exasperation getting the better of her, "it must be due any minute! It's got to be the same baby!"

The herald returned shortly with the news that the new King would be born in Bethlehem.

"There you are," said Herod to the three men, "and now you must be off to see Him." He paused. "There is just one thing. I would dearly love to visit Him too, so when you've found Him, I'd like you to come back this way and let me know exactly where He is. You wouldn't mind doing that for me, would you?"

"It'll be a great pleasure, your Majesty." The visitors bowed and left.

"A great pleasure indeed," murmured Herod, as an evil smile flickered across his flabby face, "because when I know where He is… I shall kill Him."

Queenie could feel the blood draining from her face. Kill Him? Mary's baby? That couldn't happen! She couldn't *allow* it to happen!

"That's it!" she cried, jumping up and inadvertently standing on a quail who'd fallen asleep on her shoulder. "We're getting out of here! Tonight!"

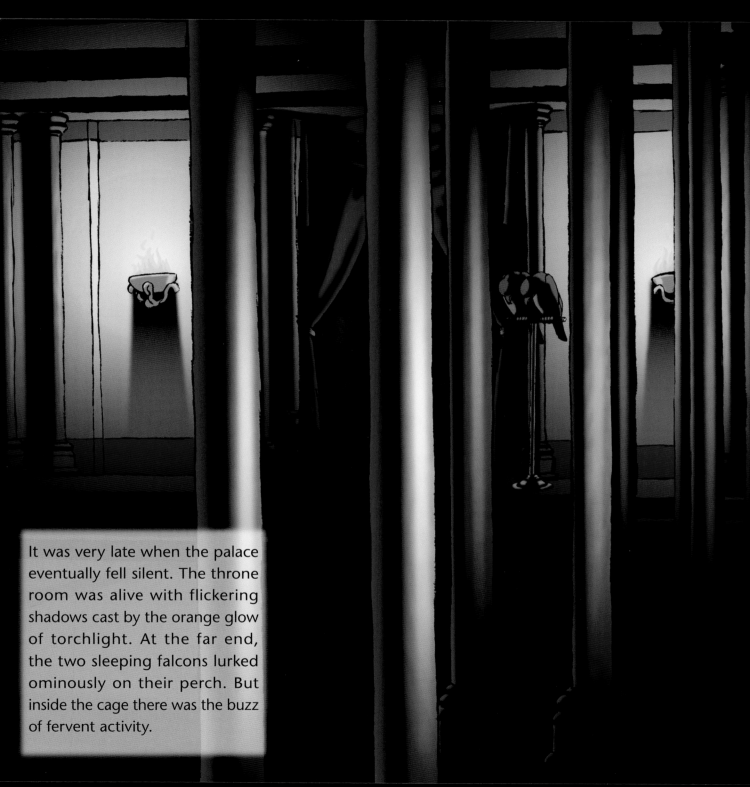

It was very late when the palace eventually fell silent. The throne room was alive with flickering shadows cast by the orange glow of torchlight. At the far end, the two sleeping falcons lurked ominously on their perch. But inside the cage there was the buzz of fervent activity.

One on top of the other, the quails had formed a tight pyramid. Bobby was balancing on the peak, trying to heave open the cage door.

"He won't budge it," whispered Tommy, wings outspread and with another quail's foot jammed uncomfortably on his head. "We've tried it loads of times before."

But Queenie was determined. "Yes, well, there are more of us now so we can push him up higher. Anyway, this time it's got to budge. This time it's a matter of life and death."

"It's always been a matter of life and death," grumbled Tommy. "Ours!"

"Oh stop moaning," she replied. "We've got to get to Mary and warn her before those three stargazers find her. If anything happens to that baby, I'll never forgive myself."

"I think I can see the problem," Bobby called down in a low voice. "There's something holding the catch closed."

"Well get rid of it!" hissed Queenie impatiently. "And do it quietly!"

Twisting awkwardly, Bobby managed to get hold of the pin that seemed to be locking the catch. He pulled hard. It didn't move. He tried again, groaning with the effort, but it was still stuck fast.

"If it won't pull, maybe it needs a push," suggested Tommy.

"I'll push *you* in a minute," muttered a disgruntled Bobby, but it was worth a try. He pulled back his head then flung it sideways at the pin, which, to his astonishment, flew out and shot up in the air.

"Catch it!" urged Queenie. If it hit the floor the noise would be certain to wake the falcons. Tommy stuck out his foot and the pin fell neatly into his claws.

"That was close," breathed Bobby.

Queenie looked at him sternly. "Too close," she said. "Now, let's try and get out of here, shall we? Quietly!"

Bobby pushed upwards against the door with his head. It was heavy, but he managed to ease it open gradually. Then, keeping a close eye on the sleeping falcons, Queenie began to usher the nervous quails out of the cage.

She was the last to claw her way out and immediately looked all round for an escape route from the palace.

"Over there!" whispered Tommy, indicating a small opening in the wall through which a shaft of moonlight had begun to trickle. Queenie's face brightened for a second, but then the anxiety returned. The opening, although high up, was right above the falcons' perch.

"Oh well," she shrugged, "we'll have to go one at a time, but it's that or nothing."

One by one, she encouraged the quails out through the window. "Not a sound! Glide!"

"This is no good," interrupted Tommy, "it'll take too long. We'll have to be next if we're ever going to get to Bethlehem."

"He's right," added Bobby, "and I don't often agree with him."

"I know," sighed Queenie. She looked round her sadly. "I just wanted to see all these others safe. But you know what to do," she said to them softly. "When you take off, just keep your eyes fixed on that window and you'll have no problem."

With that, she glanced at Tommy and said, "See you outside," to boost her confidence, spread her wings and was gone. A few moments later Tommy joined her, and a few moments after that the three of them should have been on their way to Bethlehem.

But Bobby, who'd got very fat on King Herod's plentiful food, was having trouble with his take-off and found it almost impossible to get any lift. He missed the window and lost his rhythm completely. Before he knew what was happening, he'd collided with a vase, which fell to the floor with a splintering crash.

Queenie and Tommy exchanged a horrified glance. They looked back through the window in time to see Bobby bounce head first into a bronze urn, his legs left waggling helplessly in the air.

"We've got to get him out!" shrieked Queenie. But the worst had happened. The falcons were awake.

Their eyes narrowed when they spied the quails cowering on top of the cage. They stretched out their necks and lunged. In a chaotic fluster of squawks and wings, the quails scattered as they tried to get to the window. Undeterred, the falcons separated and dived for them again.

"Don't just sit there!" Queenie screamed at Tommy. "*Do* something!" Then, with a look of utter determination, she flew straight at one of the falcons and skimmed the top of his head.

"Gotcha!" she snarled through a clenched beak. The falcon turned sharply in mid-air. Queenie was on top of the cage. He fixed her with a burning stare, opened his wings, then shot like an arrow towards her. With a huge effort, she heaved the cage door upright, then turned to face the plunging falcon. He was almost on top of her when, at the last moment, she leapt aside. Unable to change course, the falcon hit the door and fell inside the cage with a thud. Then Queenie clanged the door shut behind him.

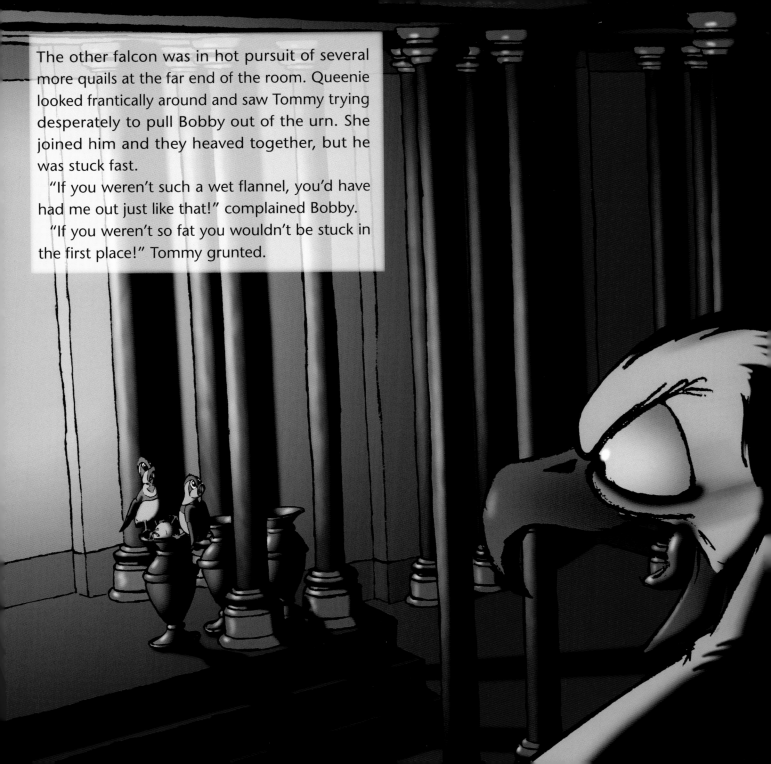

The other falcon was in hot pursuit of several more quails at the far end of the room. Queenie looked frantically around and saw Tommy trying desperately to pull Bobby out of the urn. She joined him and they heaved together, but he was stuck fast.

"If you weren't such a wet flannel, you'd have had me out just like that!" complained Bobby.

"If you weren't so fat you wouldn't be stuck in the first place!" Tommy grunted.

But the falcon had spotted them. As Queenie glanced up, he was preparing to dive.

"Er... Tommy...," she gulped. He followed her gaze. There was no time to think.

"PULL!" they screamed, and with one final, life-depending wrench, they heaved Bobby out into the air. The falcon tried to stop, but it was too late and he plummeted head first into the urn. There was an uproarious cheer from the few remaining quails. Bobby turned and saluted them.

"Do you think we can go now?" asked Queenie.
"Absolutely, boss," said Bobby.

Deep into the night the quails flew, their wings beating purposefully on the still, clear air. Some way ahead of them, a huge star was gleaming in the inky black arc of the sky.

"I'm worn out," puffed Bobby. "Can we slow down a bit?"

"No, we can't!" said Queenie, breathless but determined. "We've got to find that baby before those three sky-watchers get to him."

"But they left ages ago," Bobby complained. "They're probably there already."

Queenie ignored him. "Just keep your eyes fixed on that star" she said. "It's bigger and brighter than all the others.

It's got to be the one those men told Herod about. And if I'm right, it's set for Bethlehem."

"And what about when we get there?" added Tommy. "We still won't know where he is."

"That'll be easy," smiled Queenie. "This is the Son of God we're talking about. He'll be in a place fit for a King."

But Queenie couldn't have been more wrong. Mary and Joseph had wandered the length of Bethlehem in search of somewhere to stay, but there wasn't a room to be had. A smart-looking guesthouse down a quiet side street was their last hope. The landlord's response was the same.

"No, I'm sorry. We're full. You should have got here earlier."

Rachel, his wife, appeared in the doorway.

"What're you doing out here, Garrulus?" she snapped at her husband. "I thought I sent you to fetch some water."

"You did, my little pomegranate, you did," replied Garrulus. "But as you can see, I've been waylaid by this gentleman and his wife. I shall go now and get a bucketful."

"No, hold on." Rachel put a hand on his arm to stop him. She frowned at Joseph. "I really do think you ought to get your wife inside," she remarked sternly. "She looks as if she could give birth at any moment."

"Believe me, that's what I've been trying to do!" Joseph was exasperated. "But everywhere's full up. There's nowhere to stay."

"That's no surprise, not with this census," said Rachel. She thought for a moment. "I tell you what I'll do. I've a stable round the back. The animals are in there so it's not overly clean and it smells a bit, but at least you'll be out of the cold night air and you'll have a bit of privacy."

"Oh thank you!" sighed Mary with immense relief.

So, later that night, Mary's baby was born in a stable, not in a place fit for a king, not even in the little house in Nazareth that Mary had lovingly prepared for His arrival, and without the cradle to lie in that Joseph had carved so fondly. He had nothing but a rickety shed to shelter Him and a heap of rough straw.

"How much further?" moaned Bobby, his whole body aching with the effort of keeping up with the others. "My wings feel like a pair of old cabbage leaves!"

"They smell like a pair of old cabbage leaves too" muttered Tommy. He was exhausted as well, but wouldn't admit it.

"It can't be that far," encouraged Queenie. "We've been going a good while."

They flew over the brow of a hill. In the distance far beneath them was the warm glow of a fire, and the birds could just make out three dark shapes huddled in its flickering shadows.

"It's all right for some" mumbled Bobby, gazing down despondently. "I bet they've just made camp for the night. They're probably cooking supper on that fire, a big pot of thick stew with dumplings and crusty bread!" His beak began to water.

Queenie slowed down slightly.

"We'd better get down there," she said unexpectedly.

"Why?" asked Bobby, his eyes brightening. "Do you fancy some stew?"

"Of course I don't fancy some stew!" she snapped. "There are three of them down there, aren't there? They could be Herod's three visitors. We need to go and see."

"Good idea" agreed Tommy.

"Not as good as the stew one" Bobby sulked.

As they drew closer, they could see across the hillside quite clearly. It lay washed in the strange, glimmering light of the star they were following. There were sheep scattered up the grassy slope. The three figures round the fire had noticed the star and were gazing at it curiously.

"You know, I'm sure that star's getting closer" the birds heard one of them say. "Well it'd better not come too close," replied another, "it'll frighten the sheep."

"It's not them," said Tommy. "They must be shepherds."

"I know," Queenie sighed, her eyes heavy with disappointment. "I just thought we might have caught up with them."

"Shall we have a rest then?" asked Bobby eagerly.

"No, we shall not!" Queenie looked straight ahead, determination flooding back to her face. "We've come this far, haven't we? Nothing's going to stop us now!"

She threw her companions an encouraging glance and the three birds sped on again into the night. "Look out!" Tommy's anguished cry split the air.

But it was too late. He'd spotted the net stretched across their path but not soon enough to stop them flying into it. As they fell in a tangled, struggling heap in the dust, the shepherds spun round.

"I don't believe it!" said the shortest one, his eyes wide with amazement. "Look, Duffy! Lumpy's trap actually caught something!"

"All right, boss," muttered Bobby to Queenie, "and how do you propose we get out of *this* one?"

Lumpy was already inspecting the contents of the net.

"That's a stroke of luck," he said, "there's three – one each! Stuffed quail tonight, chaps. Duffy, you get some more wood and stoke up that fire, and Fig and I will get plucking!"

"No, hang on a minute." Fig was watching something intently. His voice was soft and almost quavering. "What in the world is that?"

Five pairs of eyes followed his gaze. There was another bright light in the sky.

"Must be a star" suggested Lumpy.

Duffy shook his head. "That's not a star," he said darkly. "It's got wings!"

There was no time to run. An angel was suddenly hovering radiantly just above them.

"I don't believe it," gasped Bobby, trying to hide his head in the dust, "it's happening again!"

"Don't be afraid!" the angel called down. But the shepherds were terrified and shuffled about, frantically trying to hide behind each other.

"Don't be afraid," he repeated. "I've come to tell you of something wonderful, something that will bring great joy to everyone in the world. The Son of God has been born in Bethlehem."

Queenie caught her breath. "I knew it! I told you, didn't I. I knew it!"

"Go and look for Him," the angel continued. "You'll find Him in a stable, a little baby wrapped up against the cold, lying in a manger."

"That doesn't sound right," Queenie frowned. "What's he doing in a feeding trough?"

"This child is a Gift for everyone," the angel announced. "Through Him all people can be saved from darkness and be close to God forever."

A faint sound of music floated on the air. It grew louder and louder until the sky was filled with angels singing at the tops of their voices, "Glory to God in the highest and peace to all people on earth!" The shepherds were transfixed.

But as suddenly as they were filled, the skies began to empty.

"No!" shouted Queenie, watching helplessly as the angels disappeared. "Don't go! King Herod wants to kill the baby! You've got to warn them!"

A light breeze lifted for a moment then dropped, and the silence of the night crept back to the shadowy hills. They were gone.

Queenie was beside herself. "What're we going to do?" she groaned, gazing at the others in despair. "We'll never get there now. How can *He* save the world if we can't save *Him*?"

The shepherds, who'd understandably forgotten all about the quails, were still staring towards the sky.

"Wow!" breathed Duffy.

"Yeah!" murmured Lumpy and Fig.

"I reckon we ought to go then," continued Duffy slowly.

"Go where?" was the vague response.

"To Bethlehem, of course," he said, "to see this baby."

"Now that's a good idea, that is," answered Fig, pulling himself together. Then a thought struck him. "I suppose we really ought to take him a present."

"What about those quails?" said Lumpy.

Fig shook his head. "Dear me, no. I'm not hungry any more."

"No, I mean as a present" replied Lumpy. "Brilliant," smiled Duffy. "You're not as daft as you look!"

With that, the shepherds threw dirt on their fire to damp down the flames, gathered up the net of quails and, with the light of the star to guide them, set off for Bethlehem.

The quails' spirits soared as they bounced along on Duffy's back.

"They're taking us right to Him," cried Bobby gleefully. "What a result!"

The shepherds didn't know Bethlehem very well, and finding the right stable in amongst the maze of narrow streets and courtyards was no easy task.

"It's here, I know it is" whispered Queenie to Bobby and Tommy. They were all very cramped inside the net but she peered about her as best she could. "Look at the star, it's right overhead."

"I think we ought to ask" Lumpy remarked.

"And what are we going to say?" scoffed Duffy curtly. "'Excuse me, we're looking for the Son of God. I don't suppose you've happened to see Him lying around in a feeding trough?' Everyone'll think we're barmy!"

"Sorry to interrupt." Rachel's voice made them jump. "I couldn't help overhearing. Are you looking for a baby?" The shepherds were slightly bewildered but managed a nod.

"You'd better follow me," she continued. "It's all been a bit of a panic, but I'm sure Mary won't mind now. I was just taking round some fresh water."

Queenie's heart thumped excitedly as Rachel led the shepherds down an alley beside the guest-house, then under an archway to a low stable building in a corner of the yard. Rachel popped her head inside the door and asked softly, "Are you up to having some visitors now?" Then she turned to the shepherds and beckoned them in. Mary was half lying on a pile of straw. In the dim light of a single lantern, she looked exhausted but very happy. Joseph was sitting beside her. When Queenie saw her, she caught her breath. All those months locked away in Herod's miserable cage, she hadn't really believed she'd ever see her again.

Tommy's voice broke into her quiet thoughts. "Well," he whispered, "we're here. What next?"

Queenie looked at him in dismay. "I don't know!" She hadn't thought that far. "I don't know how to make them understand!"

The shepherds gathered round the manger. "Ah, he's beautiful!" crooned Fig.

Duffy remembered the quails on his back. "I nearly forgot," he mumbled shyly. "We brought you a present.

It's not much, I'm afraid, but it was all a bit last minute."

"Not much?" huffed Bobby indignantly. "Charming!"

"Look at them, Joseph," said Mary, smiling delightedly, "they're just like the ones who used to come to the house." She looked at Rachel. "Can I let them out? They look so uncomfortable in there." Rachel nodded.

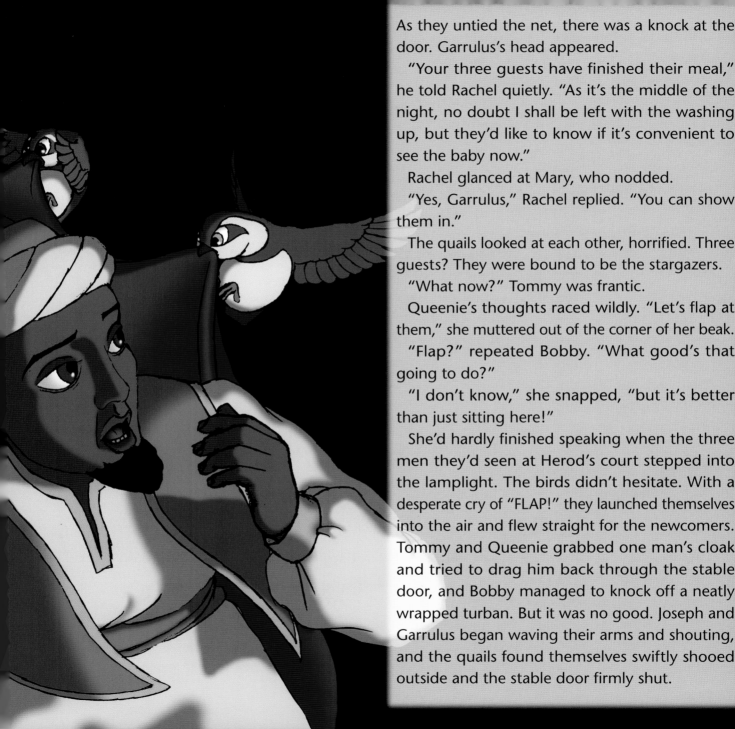

As they untied the net, there was a knock at the door. Garrulus's head appeared.

"Your three guests have finished their meal," he told Rachel quietly. "As it's the middle of the night, no doubt I shall be left with the washing up, but they'd like to know if it's convenient to see the baby now."

Rachel glanced at Mary, who nodded.

"Yes, Garrulus," Rachel replied. "You can show them in."

The quails looked at each other, horrified. Three guests? They were bound to be the stargazers.

"What now?" Tommy was frantic.

Queenie's thoughts raced wildly. "Let's flap at them," she muttered out of the corner of her beak.

"Flap?" repeated Bobby. "What good's that going to do?"

"I don't know," she snapped, "but it's better than just sitting here!"

She'd hardly finished speaking when the three men they'd seen at Herod's court stepped into the lamplight. The birds didn't hesitate. With a desperate cry of "FLAP!" they launched themselves into the air and flew straight for the newcomers. Tommy and Queenie grabbed one man's cloak and tried to drag him back through the stable door, and Bobby managed to knock off a neatly wrapped turban. But it was no good. Joseph and Garrulus began waving their arms and shouting, and the quails found themselves swiftly shooed outside and the stable door firmly shut.

"Brilliant plan that. Flap!" said Tommy disconsolately. Queenie ignored him and flew up to the roof.

"What are you doing?" he called.

Queenie had no intention of giving up now. "There must be a way back in!" As the two weary birds joined her, she'd already spotted a small hole in the roof and was peering down inside the stable.

"We'll never get through there!" said Bobby. But Queenie silenced him with a wave of her wing, watching the scene below intently.

"What's going on?" whispered Tommy. There was only room for one pair of eyes at the hole. "They're giving him presents," Queenie answered.

Tommy and Bobby put an ear each to the roof.

"I've brought you some gold," said one of the visitors.

"That's a bit flash" remarked Bobby, but he was instantly hushed by the others. "Gold is a gift for a King," the man explained to Mary.

Queenie watched as the second man laid his present amongst the straw near the manger.

"This is some frankincense," he said softly, "because you are God's Son and will be worshipped and honoured."

The final gift was of myrrh.

"I thought myrrh's what you put on dead people," Tommy commented. "What kind of present's that for a baby?"

Mary looked at the third man, puzzled.

He answered her silent question. "This myrrh is because his life will be so special. From its beginning... to its end."

"Right, that's it," said Bobby, jumping up and fluffing out his feathers, "they're on about doing him in already!"

But Queenie shook her head. "No," she urged, "I don't think that's what he means."

"Well whatever he means," Tommy said decisively, "if we don't stop them going back to Herod, that baby's had it anyway."

Queenie, still looking through the hole, let out a sudden gasp. "Oh no! They're leaving!"

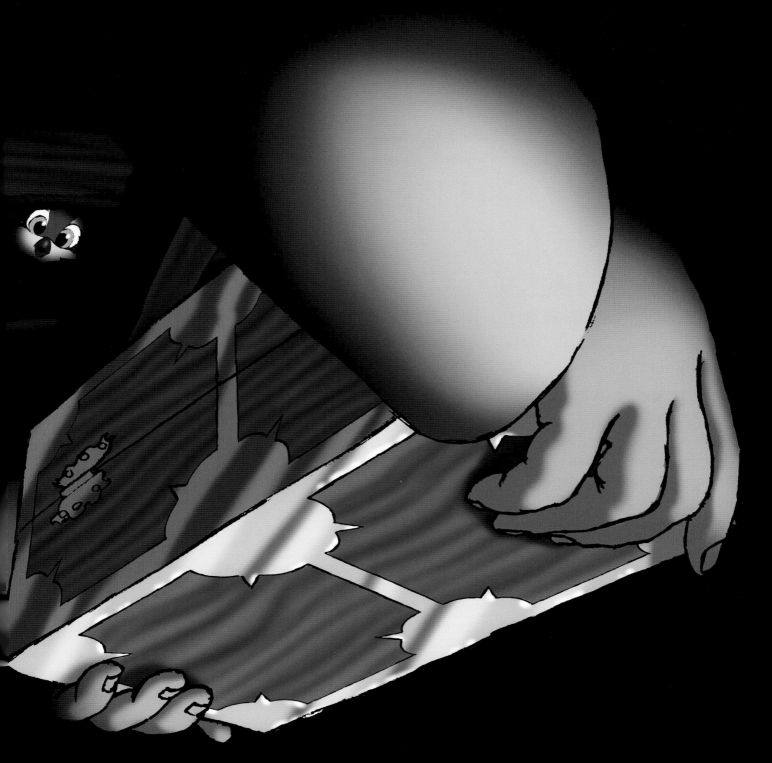

The birds looked around them desperately. There must be some way to stop them. The archway that led to the alley beside the guest-house was the only way through to the main street. Standing above it was a large decorative stone urn. Bobby spotted it first.

"There!" he shouted. "When they walk under the archway, we'll knock that urn over! We'll flatten them!"

"Don't be daft! We can't flatten them!" replied Tommy. Then he grinned mischievously. "But we can certainly give them a nasty shock!"

They flew over and perched on the urn. It was solid and cumbersome. Queenie looked despondent. "It's no good, we'll never shift this."

"We're going to have to," said Tommy. "We need more time and this is our only hope." As he finished speaking, Joseph appeared in the stable doorway with the three visitors. "Have you far to go?" he asked.

"Several weeks' journey," was the reply, "but we're in no hurry."

Listening to every word, the birds put their backs to the urn and started to push as hard as they could. It didn't shift an inch.

"Again!" hissed Tommy. Bobby grunted with the effort. Nothing seemed to happen and then all of a sudden – "Did you feel that?" he said excitedly. "I'm sure it just moved!"

"We were going to go back the way we came and let King Herod know where your baby is," one of the men was explaining to Joseph. "He was very helpful, and seemed keen to come and pay his respects."

"Respects, my tail feathers!" muttered Bobby and the urn lurched forward. Another huge push slid it precariously close to the archway's edge. The men were almost underneath.

Tommy braced himself for one final heave.

"It's strange, though," the man continued, and stopped thoughtfully. "We each had a dream warning us not to go near Herod."

The quails, their backs still against the urn, stopped in mid shove.

"So we've decided to go home a different way." There was a second's sickening silence.

"Whoops!" said Bobby, but the teetering urn overbalanced and crashed heavily down, the birds falling helplessly with it.

"Look out!" shrieked Joseph. He had barely time to push the men out of the way before it hit the ground in a great cloud of dust.

"Everyone all right?" spluttered Tommy anxiously. A pair of battered looking heads popped out of the rubble.

"Everyone's absolutely fine" Queenie glowed. Mary's baby was safe. Nothing else mattered.

"Garrulus!" Rachel's stern voice sliced through the night air. "Get out here and clean up this mess. I've told you a thousand times that's a daft place to stand a pot!"

"Come on," said Tommy, "I think it's time we went home."

"And if we leave now, we might just be in time for breakfast!" Bobby added. So when no-one was looking, the three friends flew up out of the yard, over the stable roof and began the long journey back to Nazareth. A faint, pinkish glow along the horizon had begun to chase the darkness from the sky. Dawn was breaking.

But Bethlehem was still well within their sights when Queenie called to the others to stop. They perched in a tree for a moment.

"What's the matter now?" asked Bobby.

She took a deep breath. "I want to go back."

"What for this time?" Bobby was slightly exasperated. "The baby's all right, you heard those men."

"It must have been God who warned them about Herod," added Tommy. "All our messing about and He had it under control all the time!"

"It's not that," she murmured. "I've never been anywhere as special as that stable. That little baby's here to bring life. Not just to us who've seen him, but to everyone. God's come down to earth and… I just want to say thank You."

Bobby sighed. He couldn't argue with that.

"Go on then," said Tommy kindly. "We'll wait here for you."

With a brief smile, Queenie flew back to the sleeping town of Bethlehem and the stable standing in a quiet back street.

The door was slightly open and a shaft of light streamed out across the yard. She could hear Mary singing softly to the baby Jesus. Another smile lifted the corners of her beak and, with a little shiver of happiness and anticipation, Queenie hopped inside.

It's a DVD too!

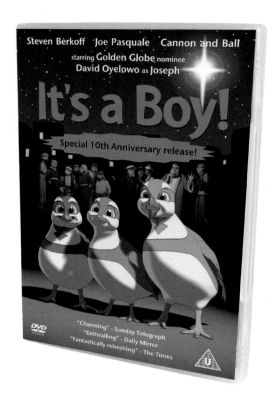

IT'S A BOY! (DVD)
Produced by Steve Legg
ISBN: 5027957-001619

Watch this amazing story of the birth of Jesus! The DVD version of the *It's a Boy!* book took three years to complete and was the idea of Steve Legg, who heads up The Breakout Trust. The film was distributed to 26,000 primary schools in the UK in 2005. 10 years on – a special 10th Anniversary edition has been created to tell the story to a new generation of children.

"This is creative, down-to-earth, funny and entertaining … it's fantastic to be part of something classy and meaningful." (Joe Pasquale, voice of Innkeeper, DVD)

"Rock on quails … You're gonna grab the world by its braces. What an honour to take part in such a sensational film" (Cannon and Ball, voices of quails Tommy and Bobby, DVD)

Available from your local Christian bookshop or direct from CWR and Steve Legg at The Breakout Trust.
01252 784700
www.cwr.org.uk/store

Dive deeper into God's Story

PENS ACTIVITY BIBLE

By Alexa Tewkesbury
ISBN: 978-1-78259-153-5

Ideal for children aged 3 to 6.
Take your *Pens* friends along and discover Bible stories, puzzles, games and activities. There is plenty to entertain and teach young children from the Old and New Testament. Each Bible story comes with two activities.

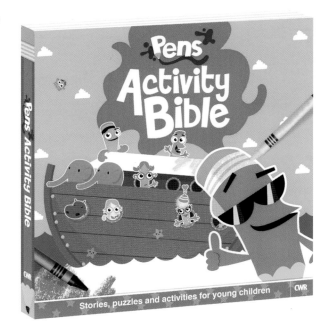

TOPZ ACTIVITY BIBLE

by Alexa Tewkesbury
ISBN: 978-1-78259-419-2

Ideal for children aged 7 to 11.
The Topz Gang retell 27 key Bible stories, bringing God's Word to life.
Readers will explore many of their favourite stories along with some lesser known, with Bible characters such as Noah, Moses, Hannah, Gideon and Jesus. Every story is followed by two *Topz* activities to challenge and entertain young readers.

Available from your local Christian bookshop or direct from CWR.
01252 784700
www.cwr.org.uk/store

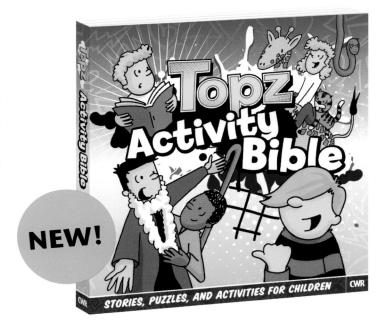

BIBLE READING NOTES

Topz is a popular bimonthly devotional for 7- to 11-year-olds. The Topz Gang teach biblical truths through daily Bible readings, word games, puzzles, riddles, cartoons, competitions and simple prayers. Available as an annual subscription (6 bimonthly issues) or as single issues.

TOPZ SECRET STORIES

The *Topz Secret Stories* are full of fun as they help readers discover things about themselves and God. They include relevant biblical insight as the rival Dixons Gang cause problems and opportunities for the Topz Gang.

TOPZ SECRET DIARIES

Take a sneak peek into the lives of each member of Topz in their *Topz Secret Diaries*. Bursting with diary entries, puzzles and things to do, this series helps readers find out more about God and their relationship with Him.

TOPZ GOSPELS

Join the whole Topz Gang on more fun adventures as they explore each Gospel as children living in Bible times.

For current prices and the full *Topz* range, visit **www.cwr.org.uk/topz**